Berlin Passages

Berlin Passages, Cultural Mapping and Transdisciplinary Explorations in Urban Space

Notes between Field Diary and Poetry

Joachim Broecher

Notes on the cover photo:

This photo shows two BVG[1] subway trains at *Krumme Lanke* station in Berlin-Zehlendorf. I chose these as a motif because the metropolitan research attempted here would not be feasible, or even imaginable, without the excellent public transport network available to us in Berlin. The subway trains in particular play a special role in this research. The subway is in equal measure the setting, subject matter, method and medium.

Bibliographic information for the German National Library:

The German National Library lists this publication in the German National Bibliography; detailed bibliographic data are available on the Internet at http://dnb.dnb.de

© 2023 Joachim Broecher

English translation: The Translation People, Bonn, Germany

German version, BoD – Books on Demand, 2022

Design and printing by BoD – Books on Demand, Norderstedt, Germany

ISBN: 978-3-7578-4521-6

---

[1] Berliner Verkehrsbetriebe

Table of Contents

Theoretical Background and Scientific Method

Berlin offers diverse spaces for reflection and for the transformation of social reality. At the same time, these places offer the reconceptualization of a different economic, social, pedagogical and cultural reality. Just as it did in the 19th century, since the fall of the *Berlin Wall*, the city has held the status of a creative, dynamic and dazzling metropolis – comparable to New York, London or Paris. The multi-layered, creative city captivates people from all over the world by creating space for the development of identities and lifestyles. We can read about such notions in the letters of Alfred Kerr (1997), for example. During the Weimar Republic - Peter Gay (2002) and Robert Beachy (2015) reconstructed and documented these developments very vividly - social tensions, which of course exist beyond the *creative class* (Florida, 2002, 2005), do not seem to slow down the innovative power of Berlin as a metropolis.

The environment we are observing in Berlin now can hypothetically be seen as a *hothouse* for future social developments. My own theoretical and scientific work was initially very much an examination of pedagogical experiences I had gathered in educational institutions (e.g. Broecher, 2000, 2015c, 2016, 2019a,b, 2022b; Broecher, Davis et al., 2014; Broecher, Painter et al., 2017). The work was relatively narrow in scope until I began to make Berlin the center of my world in 2015. In the free atmosphere of this metropolis, I arrived at models of thinking that reopened, rearranged and expanded everything that had gone before (Bröcher, 2021a,c,e,g), including a critical review of the knowledge and the politics of knowledge in the field of emotional and social learning in and beyond schools (Bröcher,

2021b). At the same time, I revived background experiences from earlier contexts, that seemed to be forward-looking (Broecher 2015a,b, 2019d; Bröcher, 2021f, Broecher, Davis, and Painter, 2017; Toczyski et al., 2022).

After this, I began to write an entirely new and different kind of work. I was now concerned with social transformation – not just with creating more quality in individual social or educational fields. These new concepts were also part of the impetus that led me to spend time in more rural areas, where, together with my family, I acquired a 19th century farmstead. We are now in the process of developing this and converting it into a think tank (Broecher, 2023a,b; Broecher and Painter, 2023). Without the growth mindset gained in the metropolis of Berlin, however, things would not have come to this. In this way, the roles of urban and rural spaces are now being placed in a higher context. The crucial question is: How will people of the future learn, work and live?

But the focus of this book – the German version was published a year earlier (Bröcher, 2022a) - is the urban space of the metropolis: *Berlin*. If we take as inspiration Walter Benjamin's *The Arcades Project* (1999), which is based on extensive explorations in the metropolis of 1920s and 1930s Paris, and undertake something similar, we have to translate this into today's experience. That is, if we transfer this idea of interdisciplinary exploration to the discovery of the metropolis Berlin, we would now have to utilize other means of documentation and analysis than those preferred by Benjamin. Benjamin, were he alive now, might choose a hybrid form of book, diary, blog, or video channel, etc. We would probably find him on YouTube, Instagram, and maybe even TikTok. Perhaps he would also have tried to integrate fragmentary linguistic forms – poetry, etc. into a contemporary version of *The Arcades Project*; forms in a way also related to hip hop and rap.

Neither the encyclopedic breadth produced by Benjamin, nor the systematic nature that he gave *The Arcades Project*, can be attainable goals nowadays, in view of the abundance and differentiation of today's knowledge – especially in the realms of the Internet, virtual databanks, and everything digital. Nowadays, it is unlikely that someone would be able to describe, analyze, and create such interconnections of knowledge in an all-encompassing way for the 21st century, like Benjamin did, or at least attempted, for the 19th century.

In the present book, I therefore want to keep the amount of text manageable, and even offer a rather minimalistic account; entirely directing my efforts into lyric poetry that creates a series of images, merging them into a whole, as in an impressionist painting. Of course, I cannot claim completeness or representativeness of my written and printed words; indeed, I could easily fill 500 pages with the material from the seven years I spent doing fieldwork in Berlin.

In the context of this work, I am inspired by poems penned by Wisława Szymborska, Czesław Miłosz, and Zbigniew Herbert, also by the works of Dorota Masłowska. I came upon the works of these poets through research on the emotional and social geographies of Polish literature, in the sense of opening up spaces of reflection and transformation.

Building on earlier socio-cultural explorations of Berlin (Bröcher, 2021d; Broecher and Painter, 2019, 2021), I now link all of this, in a transdisciplinary sense, with qualitative social research (e.g., Denzin and Lincoln, 2011), field research (e.g., Burgess, 1991), urban research, cultural mapping (e.g., Duxbury et al., 2015; Roberts, 2012), and emotional and social geographies (e.g., Davidson et al., 2017), to name only the most important methods and concepts I use here. I also tie it into theoretical models, for example to Sloterdijk's *Spheres trilogy* (2011, 2014, 2016), in particular his suggestive *Theory of Foams* to describe contemporary society, or to Richard Sennett's sociological studies and designs revolving around the *Design of Disorder* (e.g., Sendra and Sennett, 2020; Sennett, 1992). I would also be amiss not to cite *The Arcades Project*, in connection with Benjamin's epochal work.

My method is, however, in a way unsystematic, subjective and coincidental. I mix the times, the decades; the past with the present. Paul Feyerabend (2010) certainly influenced me, with his book *Against Method: Outline of an anarchistic theory of knowledge*. Ultimately, it is my hope that despite the method, a manner of overall picture emerges. In the texts documented here, I gauge ways in which the subjective appropriation of urban spaces takes place in the *creative city* that is Berlin. On the one hand this is done on the basis of currently-known research methods in the social sciences, but on the other, the approach is unconventional and transcends boundaries – both the literary and transdisciplinary. How can we explore new territory if we do not attempt something new? There can be no direct 1:1 application of that which we have discovered or clarified in pedagogy, society or culture; things are too complex, too subtle, too stubborn for this, but herein also lies their allure.

Joachim Broecher, Berlin, Juli 2023

Nightly Film Seminar on Hipster Bar

He gives me an
extra bedspread to lay
underneath, as the futon
I'll be sleeping on

is hard as a
board; the guest before
me quickly left again,
but I stay; outside

the window, yellow and
on the minute, the
overhead train shoots upward
as if I were

in north Manhattan; under
the balcony a hipster
bar full of young
people, many of them
standing outside, laughing, smoking;

the smell of hashish
permeates through the high
white balcony door; next
door, behind the white

double door, a kind
of private movie theater,
with some real cinema
seats, *movie night in*

Prenzlauer Berg, my host
says, inviting me to
join him, but after
the flight and all

of that, my body
longs for the futon,
despite everything; women with
highly toupeed black hair

with rhinestones in it
are the guests; they
interrupt the films, discuss,
smoke, drink wine, the

night stays warm, downstairs
in the hipster bar
electro beats, rattling overhead
trains, clouds of hashish.

Alfred Döblin's Berlin *Underworld*

I stroll through the
featureless apartment blocks, behind
Alexanderplatz, where I live
these days, and think

of Alfred Döblin's Berlin
novel and how everything
has changed; the dark
courtyards plowed up, the

narrow alleys, the dive
bars, the slaughterhouses, the
whole shadowy world in
which prostitutes, pimps, thieves,

dealers loiter; suddenly a
crack widens in a
wall, and I go
in, I descend, into

the darkness, only sparsely
lit; on a bar
stool a *Bacchus* with
a hairy thick belly,

in leather harness, with
a younger companion next
to him; drinks are
served at a dimly

lit counter; to the
side in a row,
a slim man, he
could well have been

a lecturer at a
university of the 80s,
or one of the
activists of the *Wilhelm*

Reich Society, handing out
flyers; he crouches down
and serves a man,
who, breathing increasingly fast,

bends backward and leans
against the wall, while
three or four men
are already lined up,

waiting, perhaps even feverish;
down a staircase, labyrinthine
corridors, to the sides,
lost in jet-black darkness,

then the metallic clink
of a chain; behind
iron cage bars, dimly
lit, moves a pink

mountain of flesh, gleaming
murkily out of the
darkness, chained in the
cage, crouching on all

fours, a metal ring
around its fat neck;
a man approaches the
cage and presses his

loins against the metal
bars, chains rattling, rapid
breathing, the pink mound
of flesh rises, then

a smacking of the
lips; out of the
darkness steps a powerful
bear, as if drawn

by George Grosz, his
pants down to his
knees; I slam Döblin's
book closed again, and

make myself tea, in
my standardized prefabricated apartment.

The *Metropol Theater* at *Nollendorfplatz*

Even just the view
out of the window
on this bombastic facade
and a little historical

research on the *Metropoltheater,*
at the *Nollendorfplatz*, make
it clear, what a
pulsating place of the

1920s this is, where
I have rented a
room; roaring, long nights,
glamour, glitter, experimental spaces

for identities, redesigning of
lifestyles; my host from
South America, a photographer
and city guide, now

Airbnb became his business
model; chats in the
evenings, on platforms; he
sleeps behind a wall

of books, in the
living-dining-kitchen space
I have to cross
to get to my

room; fried eggs after
fitness training are available
only until 9.30 p.m.

The Weavers or: Missed Opportunities for Change

Alfred Kerr, born in
Breslau in 1867, spent
most of his life
in Berlin, as a

theater critic and essayist;
he was an intimate
connoisseur of Berlin's cultural
world and finer society,

especially as enjoyed in
West Berlin; people promenaded,
invited each other to
receptions, and met in

the theaters, which were
then the center of
social life; we can
read Kerr's letters from

the imperial capital, written
from 1895 to 1900,
published under the title
Wo liegt Berlin? On

1ˢᵗ January 1895, Kerr
writes: *West Berlin, this*
elegant small town in
which live those people

who can do something,
who are something, and
who have something and
imagine three times as

much as they can,
are, and have, and
further, says: *Every theater*
has its particular circle

of listeners, noted on
20ᵗʰ January 1895, *a*
certain set of people
are to be seen at

all premieres with regularity;
the more important theatrical
events cannot take place
without certain lawyers, certain

theatrical agents, certain bankers,
certain female artists, certain
publishers being present, he
writes this on the

same day, and then?
The only question of
interest, whether the Emperor
would be there, whether

he would come, or
not, it seems curious,
but in reality, things
in Germany are now

such that the entire
fate of a work
of art and of
an artist can be

significantly influenced by the
degree of attention shown
to him by the
Emperor, Kerr noted on

3rd February 1895, and
a little further on:
Thus, it would be
Interesting to see what

Impression a performance of
The Weavers would make
on the Emperor; unfortunately,
this is not possible

at present, because the
Deutsches Theater is boycotted
by court circles precisely
due to this play.

Gerhard Hauptmann's play
was published in 1892;
a drama exploring the
weavers' uprising of 1844,

a fierce literary rebellion
against the exploitation, dependence
and poverty of the
working classes, the performance

was initially banned by
the Berlin police department;
in 1893, the Administrative
High Court of Berlin

lifted the ban; in
1894 the first public performance
took place at the *Deutsches*
Theater; we know well

enough that Wilhelmine Germany
fell due to the
lack of will to
reform among its political

elite; if everything had
turned out differently, what
if, considering the social
importance that the theater

had at that time,
the imperial court had
engaged with *The Weavers*?

Lost Places and Ice Bathing

They go about in
threes, he tells me
in the warmth of
the sauna; they climb

up or abseil down,
if necessary, over fences
and walls; the allure
of the forbidden, the

hidden and the mysterious
drives them; they bathe
all year round in
the *Schlachtensee*, but especially

in winter; *ice bathing
is the best*, says
he, a young man
of about 23 years

old, who grew up
in Berlin-*Steglitz*, when
asked what is his
strongest connection to Berlin?

Alexanderplatz and *Palace of the Republic*

I remember exchanging *Westmarks*
for *Ostmarks*; it was
June 1981, a certain
amount for that one

day; I slept on
an air mattress in
the student digs of
an older school friend;

he was subletting from
an Australian journalist in
Steglitz, and the journalist
always had a younger

man with him, who
shared the room; my
friend studied literature and
sociology at the *Free*

University; his paperbacks were
carefully lined up on
a plain wooden shelf;
one evening we went

to an old cinema,
to a jazz concert
with Charlie Mariano and
Eberhard Weber; at that

time, these were big
things, if you came
from a small town
or village in West

Germany like I did;
I passed one of
the checkpoints into the
east of the city,

and when I arrived
at *Alexanderplatz* and got
off the *S-Bahn*, a
warm, heavy summer rain

fell; I took in
my hand my *Jesus
sandals*, as we called
these flip-flops back

then; I had acquired
them in Morocco during
an *Interrail* tour, perhaps
in Tangier or in

Marrakech, and walked barefoot
across *Alexanderplatz*, which was
flooded with warmth; in
the department store there,

I bought with the
Ostmarks a biography of
Rosa Luxemburg; later I
went for a coffee

and a cigarette in
the *Palace of the*
Republic, looked through the
copper-tinted windows outside,

saw the wreath of
corn, hammer and compass,
mirror-inverted on the
glass wall; I had

just passed my *Abitur*
examination in West Germany;
now it was a
question of further prospects,

of study plans, possible
places to study; on
the *Intercity* train through
the GDR, there were

guards at every door;
an almost surreal experience
by today's standards; the
philosophical and sociological literature

on the *Ikea* shelf
of the old school
friend and still young
FU[2] student; the path

I then took, the
role theory played in
it, the diverse subjects,
then in Cologne; finally,

the path to pedagogic
practice, and the various
fields therein, and ultimately,
the way back to

theory, then the reconceptualizations,
the exceedances, the expansions,
the transformations; it seems
to me that all

this has a lot
to do with this
trip to Berlin in
June 1981.

---

[2] Free University, i.e. Freie Universität Berlin

Food Revolution or: The *Edible* City

Museum of Decorative Arts,
Berlin, in May; the
future of urban food;
experimental thinking and design

concepts for alternative urban
farming methods, for different,
more sustainable food production;
urban gardening on roofs,

in-farming, vertical farming; fish
that fertilize lettuce; digitally
mapped, publicly accessible fruit
trees in Berlin and

elsewhere; the *Princess Gardens*
at the Kreuzberg *Moritzplatz*;
exploring possibilities; fishbowl discussions
with experts, moderated by

Wilfried Bommert, to start
a performance by Zack
Denfeld from the *Center
for Genomic Gastronomy*, spicy

ham on the appetizers,
from Portuguese pigs living
in an oak forest,
served in the warm

evening breeze on the
terrace, which opens onto
Potsdamer Platz; Zack designs
our bodies as food

for wolves and worms
when we live no
more, and for microorganisms
and small animals, such

as moths, that live
on our tears.

The *Holy Grail* of the Techno World

An inflatable *Berghain* facade,
as part of an
art performance, in Holland,
re-staging, thematization and processing

of the experience of
being rejected at the
door to the *Holy
Grail* of the Berlin

techno world; Dan Brown-
trained readers soon have
the key to this
magical door in their

hands; the photographs that
the door guard takes,
give insights into his
personal world of imagination,

which he recreates night
after night, like a
film director, through his
door policy; a surreal

world unfolds, as if
from the dark net,
in black and white,
slowed down, whimsical, men,

women, bodies, naked, partly
tattooed, partly disturbing, irritating,
provocative, with echoes of
Happening and *Fluxus*, a

play with social deviance;
identities developing away from
social norms, designs, states
of mind, hiding, yet

gleaming through longings; whoever
credibly embodies this world,
should easily gain access
seeing the stern gaze

of the doorman shift
to mild approval; but
this world of the
imagination, in the continuous

reenactment of which so
many want to participate,
even actually one's own
desire, or would it

even be more reasonable,
more coherent and more
sensible, to give creative
expression to one's own

ideas and longings, just
as they are, wherever
and however, and which
in turn could be

a central part of Sven
Marquardt's[3] philosophy?;
and what makes the
whole thing so ambivalent,

so appealing, so nerve-racking,
Jean-Paul Sartre, if he
were still alive, would
certainly have given us

a detailed analysis of
the play between the
door guard and the
one who feverishly seeks

entry into the *Holy
Grail* of the techno
world, given this; this
intense moment when two

---

[3] legendary bouncer of the techno club *Berghain*

worlds of imagination meet
in a gaze and
cross-reference one another, is
in the end perhaps

more significant and insightful
than the entrance into
the magical techno temple
or the rejection itself.

Schöneberg: Romeo on Roller Skates

He comes from *Brandenburg*;
my room is completely
filled with a four-poster
bed, framed with dark

red satin; he massages
a male clientele, a
special technique; he trains
his strong calves by

roller skating, in the
bathroom, perfume bottles lined
up in a row,
gifts from his ex;

the mood is still
stricken; the doctor from
the Balkans had affairs
and then left altogether,

finally moved out; *Airbnb*
appeared as a solution
to plug the financial
hole; we cook together,

talk about life, about
relationships, and about crises;
he follows the events
on his social platforms

in cinema format on
the wall of the
living room, where he
also sleeps; he shows

me the dense network
of communication that surrounds
him, contact requests, relationship
offers, men who want

a date, from time
to time also more,
but he is looking
for real commitment; we

stand on his balcony,
above *Courbièrestraße*, he smokes
thoughtfully and we stand
there silently.

Beyond Educational Institutions

We may perhaps have
to be in Neukölln
to encounter such ideas,
Systemzwang und Selbstbestimmung[4] could

be the headline here,
this is the title
of a book by
Hartmut von Hentig from

the 60s of the
last century; I found
myself an *Airbnb* on
Sonnenallee; a tangle of

names, official and unofficial,
on the papers, on
the street, at the
top of the apartment

---

[4] "System Constraints and Self-Determination" (untranslated as a published work)

door; a young man
from Venice checks me
in, into the shared
room of an acquaintance,

who is traveling through
South America; we chat
about the creative scene
in Berlin; then I

meet an engineering student
from Ohio; this, too,
turns into a longer
exchange of ideas, about

studying and life, then
I first unpack my
things, go shopping for
a few odds and

ends, enjoy the Mediterranean
atmosphere on the *Sonnenallee*;
while I make myself
something to eat in

the kitchen; I meet
a third communal apartment
resident; after her critical
school experience at a

Hamburg high school she
says, she then spent
a year traveling through
Sweden and spent time

hosted by a variety
of ventures, some of
which she also worked
on; now, in Berlin,

where she has been
for some time, she
is on the lookout
for initiatives and projects

that are designed by
people who see themselves
as free, autonomous, independent
creators, far from institutional

educational contexts; bachelor's and
master's degrees, modularized courses
of study, exams, credits,
certificates, all of this

for the young woman
who is in her
early 20s is highly
off-putting and it is

completely out of the
question to enter into
this; she is in
search of freedom and

for her, it is
all about seeing how
people think, communicate, reflect
and develop themselves and

make a difference; I
tell her that universities,
at least humanities faculties,
once also pursued the

idea of such freedom
and that I, in
my university pedagogical work
would try to somewhat

revive this idea of
freedom, despite all the
current systemic constraints; but
her distrust of the

institutions remains; she considers
my attempts to be
an isolated phenomenon; in
any case, she has

found promising traces in
Berlin, projects that speak
to her idea of
freedom, that she will

pursue next, for her
field studies.

The Old *Prussia* in the Schools

There we sit, in
the time-honored walls
of the *Zehlendorf Gymnasium*,
the coaches for the

highest pedagogical leadership offices,
at the Berlin schools,
but the assiduousness, and
the obedience, that reign

here on the one
hand and the institutionally
underpinned self-confidence, indeed
dominance and authority, on

the other; I in
fact wanted to run
a school in this
town, and I wanted

to leave behind the
presumed privilege of the
ivory tower, also its
impositions and remoteness from

reality, to return to
the professional world, from
which I had come,
a school in a

multicultural hotspot; where preliminary
discussions at grassroots and
the middle level of
school supervision could expect

good things, but the
stakeholders at the levels
of training, coaching, staff
development, and recruiting disseminate

a *Prussian* atmosphere of
subordination, conformity, discipline and
self-disciplining, only then to
expose oneself to a

constant hierarchical and lateral
evaluation and control; school
management appears here as
a management-based implementation

balancing act related to
a dense network of
legal regulations, curricular guidelines,
ministerial decrees and regulations

that are defined down
to the last detail;
this is not how
I remembered the field

of work in which
I have been involved
until a good decade
ago in West Germany;

Yes, there was once
a principal here in
Berlin, who thought he
could run his school

as a free philosopher,
and the actually retired
head of a grammar
school, but who has

found here in these
seminars a new field
of action, a space,
right at the top

of the Berlin school
system, in which he
can now fully develop
himself, now he looks

over at me, meaningfully:
How long do you
think he has been
the principal?; rhetorical question,

warm early summer air
seeping through the open
windows; I think of
taking my stand-up paddling

board and cycling to
the *Schlachtensee*; my personal
Berlin stands for freedom,
wide-open spaces, self-determination,

I say to myself,
but this here is
a new version of
the *Prussian* state school.

Micropolitics in the *Ivory Towers*

I walk through the
narrow corridors, parallel to
the railway line; the
low ceilings already push

down on you here,
and I stand at
8.00 a.m. in front
of this commission, with

my seven posters that
I have hung on
the unfolded board and
that I have digitally

sent to the commission
in advance for them
to review, graphic representations
with text modules, against

whose background I, rather
freely, want to describe
the theoretical landscapes under
debate and analyze them,

in order to make
the resultant deductions and
suggestions for the substantive
formulation of the advertised

professorship; the idea is
simultaneity, and not the
restless, volatile succession of
dozens of changing *PowerPoint*

slides with the usual
little morsels, after the
bullet points; procession-like, the
oversized commission moves into

the room; there are
no students at this
early hour of the
morning; two women complain

initially about the seven
posters I have hung
in this particular way;
they *feel downright exhausted*

by the visual complexity
of these knowledge maps,
they retort; I have
only twenty minutes for

my lecture and must
first of all deal
with this gauntlet that
has been boldly thrown;

justify myself and give
explanations, before I can
even begin to present
anything and then put

a brave face on
the matter, in order
not to turn these
ladies still further against

me; and this after
an almost sleepless night
in Berlin-*Mitte*; somewhere
behind the Museum of

Natural History, I rented
a room for a
few days via *Airbnb*
from an Italian artist

with whom I had
quite stimulating conversations, only
he woke me up
at one in the

morning, when he had
returned from a meeting
with friends and flooded
my room with light;

then there were the
three men in the
apartment next door, who
spent the whole night

playing cards and drinking
beer behind the thin
prefabricated wall, so that
I knew their scores

so well that I
could almost have played
along; a shower, yes,
a breakfast, yes, and

another extra large black
coffee at the S-Bahn
station Friedrichstraße, that too;
and now *this*; right

after the lecture, when
there was only a
little time left, come
the objections; my extensive

school experience is of
no interest at all,
although this is actually
primarily about teacher training

courses; a female professor
who had just been
appointed at another university,
here she now acts

as a so-called *external
expert*, is seemingly predestined
to ask me every
few minutes bitingly about

any third-party funds I
have raised, or to
reproach me for not
having raised such, and

about when they would
finally come, while I
say for the third
time that I have

not raised any; so
this is how professorships
are filled in the
ivory towers of Berlin,

well then, take your leave.

Escape the Ordinary, in *Prenzlauer Berg*

This stakeholder of the
creative city, living between
New York, Tel Aviv and Berlin,
embodies cosmopolitan life, like

no other; he develops
apps, has success; the
small apartment in Prenzlauer Berg,
as inspiring as if

I were immersed in
Proust's great novel about
the search for lost
time; mysterious and dark,

the hallway with its
electric seven-arm chandelier, the
room with its gigantic
bathtub on a high

pedestal; classical music automatically
playing in the bathroom;
the bed, red, plush,
wide, arranged for all

imaginable debauchery, a shelf
of wigs, for experiments
with one's own identity,
in Berlin club nights.

The *Real* University in the Subways

Sometimes I take a
book and ride the
subway with it; most
recently with Thoreau's *Walden*,

in the U 2, U 3
or U 7, for an
hour or a half-day;
a new way of

exercising my professorship, now
that universities, not only
in Berlin, are more
bureaucratic apparatuses where module

catalogs are administered, and
universes shaped by micropolitics,
where people, who need
such stages, can play

out their intrigues and
power games, while students,
are often absent; I
prefer to be outside

in the city; the
university is here, among
the people who read,
look, think, explore, have

experiences, go about the
day with open eyes
and receptive senses; I
drive through Berlin and

give stimuli through the
book that I hold
in my hand; I
read a few sentences

of Thoreau and what
he wrote around 1850
in seclusion at *Walden Pond*
in Massachusetts; about existence

and the increasingly accelerated
and alienated society, and
I listen for the clatter
on the tracks, to

the rhythmic, metallic, beguiling
beating of the wheels;
I see the people,
I hear the rhythmic

beating, I follow my
stream of thought, so
it goes on and
on; the bright orange

Penguin paperback with the
inscription *Walden* catches people's
attention, albeit cautiously, indirectly,
in that it represents

a mental point of
reference, brings perspectives into
play and opens them
up; in the crowds

between *Kottbusser Tor* and
Görlitzer Bahnhof, conversations about
reading develop; also about
reading in the subway,

and finally, about Thoreau's
Walden; another time I
take Kerouac's *On the Road,*
and yet another time

Sartre's *Being and Nothingness*;
thus I begin my
exploratory trip with the
Berlin subways once again

and mostly unforeseen situations
arise, with surprising encounters.

Vintage and Sharing on *Karl-Marx-Allee*

The young student collects
vintage furniture; from her
room I look down
on one of the

Friedrichshain cemeteries; gravestones under
the trees that throw
shade, a room for
poets and melancholics; on

the other side the
magnificent buildings from the
Soviet era; a shared
flat of perhaps eight

young people; one after
the other rents out
his or her room
for a few days

and then sleeps at
one of the others';
posters in the kitchen
advertise sharing as a

life philosophy and speak
for free love; with
the friends, who then
also join, it gets

even more crowded in
the meantime, in the
kitchen and in the
bathrooms; I have engaging

conversations, at the kitchen
table, about society, its
potential changes and about
life, especially with a

young woman from Ohio,
who took a trip to
Berlin, and then just
stayed here; now she

lives with the student
in whose vintage room
I am staying.

The *S-Bahn* and the Stream of Consciousness

Everything continues to develop,
including the associative play
with words, at times
randomly combined with each

other, in Friederike Mayröcker's
writing workshop, which can
give rise to entirely
new contexts of meaning,

or linguistic forms that
at first pose a
riddle; she embarks at
the *S-Bahn* station *Feuerbachstraße*,

stands almost motionless at
one of the doors,
and associates half sentences
and words, carefully articulated,

into the carriages, pauses
skilfully, speaks rhythmically, about
South American dictatorships, vegetarians,
the former German capital

Bonn, a pale, skinny
child-woman, black hair, red
eyes, a cup of
small change in her

hand; the language, the
consciousness, the stream of
thought, one's own, and
the external input, I

think, the life of
others and the life
conditions that envelop everything,
and the grand whole,

the unfathomable, endless universe
in which we live.

The Old *Neukölln* before Gentrification

The old Neukölln is
still alive, for instance
in the Weserstraße; where
else can we still

find these particular bars,
this patina and the
creativity; I come here
in the evening from

Sonnenallee, this oriental world,
classical music spills out
of the open windows,
the evening is warm,

like on the Mediterranean;
inside works of art
and piles of books,
a piano, the rooms

packed, a collector whose
estate is being sold;
he has lived in
New York and certainly

had a special eye
for the male body;
the owner of the
store, who came in

the early 80s from
Iran to Berlin, in
order to study painting
at the *Hochschule der*

Künste[5], runs an art
Café here that is
also a gallery, a
venue for readings, discussions,

activities and cinema evenings;
we chat a little
about turning points, and
the former perspectives in

our lives, and about
Berlin; what he does
in his project stands
for the *freedom of*

art in the world;
whether all this will
survive the wave of
gentrification, he doesn't know.

---

[5] now the Berlin University of the Arts (Universität der Künste Berlin)

Exploring *Fuggerstraße*

A dingy entrance to
a house, situated between
the trendy bars, with
a jumble of names;

finally, a beaming young
man with a southern
German accent opens the
door, leads me into

his realm; the walls
are painted black, metal
furniture, lockers like those
seen in a factory;

my bed a steel
construction, it could hold
three weightlifters, metal eyelets
on the posts, the

sides, at the top
and the bottom; on
the wardrobe a black
leather outfit, officers' leather

peaked caps, leather boots,
with high legs and
edged metal heels; *do
I want a beer?*

my host settles down
in socks on the
sofa set in the
living-dining room, an

invitation to chat which
I accept; a *Berliner Kindl*[6];
the third-born son
after two other boys,

studies event management and
has created for himself
a special source of
income, and at the

same time a personally
exciting field of experience;
he teaches men who,
in terms of age,

could be his father,
obedience, humility, submissiveness, and
how to beg for
fulfillment of the most

---

[6] a type of Berlin beer

intimate desires; we talk
with seldom experienced openness
about the emotional components,
but also the thrill

of sadomasochistic relationship constellations,
the role of leather
clothing, of military-style high
boots, peaked caps radiating

authority, and other props;
even the bathroom is
painted all black; when
appropriate, my host rents

by the day via
Airbnb, as he is
now; in a few
days, right after I

check out, he'll be
flying to the UK
to a *client* he
met at an event

in Berlin; *how does
he switch from this
friendly, radiant manner to
authoritarian, dominant behavior?* I

ask him; *Oh, that's
quite easy,* he says,
and smiles at me,
holding his gaze longer

than is usual, as
if he wants to
see whether I too
will abandon self-control; well,

that's exactly the kind
of thing he specializes
in; I leave the
door to my room

open, sleep well, but
it's hard not to
think of the things
my host hinted at.

Outside Observer at *Berghain*

Meditating in public places,
choosing these purposefully, but
without commentating on them
further; they come to

Berghain; I sit in
the early evening near
the entrance and they
ask me about my

observations and experiences, from
when and where exactly
the famous *queue* stands,
where the bouncers position

themselves, to then determine
where *Daria*, from the
Ukraine, in her orange
suit, will place herself

on the meditation cushion;
her companion will film
her during this activity
and post the video

on *Facebook; Outside Observer*
want to make people
aware of things and
provide impetus.

Thomas Bernhard and the Discourse in the Subway

Who reads Thomas Bernhard's
book *Gargoyles*[7] in the
subway?; there stands this
young man, engrossed in

the dense crowd; we
are swept away, swaying,
along the tracks, metallic
banging, clattering, the warm

air, as if this
were an *A-train*
in Manhattan; something captivates
me about this scene,

I remember my own Bernhard
readings; when he stops
reading, I talk to him;
he comes from China,

---

[7] original German title of the book: *Die Verstörung*

is studying at the
Free University[8] and has
specialized in Thomas Bernhard
as his core focus;

he considers the theme
of freedom to be
the central key element
in Bernhard's books;

we speak for a
long time, among the
many people on the
subway platform, under the

Alexanderplatz, yes freedom, I
think, and literature, what
a glimmer of hope,
embodied, I am thinking,

by this young man
from China with such
literature in his luggage,
liberating him.

---

[8] Freie Universität Berlin

Margot Honecker in the *Bear's Den*[9]

Today's educational federalism is
the root of much
social evil in Germany,
says the man, who

is now over 80
years old, who played
an important role in
the GDR education system;

in my *Airbnb* accommodation
it is not very
restful at that point
so I go to

the nearest bar and
sit on a free
stool, and order a
beer, in *Prenzlauer Berg*;

---

[9] *Bärenhöhle* is a bar in Prenzlauer Berg

the man talks a
lot about the past,
the lost, the much
better, more beautiful times;

he orders beer and
schnapps in turn, and
again and again invokes
Margot Honecker, whose unified

pedagogy we should take
example from today, then
everything would be different
and better in this

country; he staggers to
the toilet; when he
comes back, he has
somehow hit his head,

blood is running down
his temple; the bartender
makes an effort to
take care of his

injured regular; in his
apartment a cat waits
for him.

Summer Life on the *Schlachtensee*

On hot days the
S 1 is crowded with
people from the city
center who want to

cool down in the
Schlachtensee[10] or in the
Wannsee[11]; a blond young
man with a Dutch

accent passes on his
insider knowledge to me,
how to get from
the place, where I

have chained my bike,
into the water easily
and safely; in the
center of the lake

---

[10] *Schlachtensee* is a popular swimming lake in the southwest of Berlin
[11] *Wannsee* is certainly the largest and most popular lake in southwest Berlin; there you
   have opportunities for numerous water sports activities

a wooden boat, motionless,
noiseless, the oars retracted,
a formation of young
people, lying down; in

the middle a young
man reminiscent of Patricia
Highsmith's *Talented Mr. Ripley*;
on the shore, steady

drum music, as if
I were drifting here
on the *Ganges* and
closer to eternity than

ever before; stretched out
on my stand-up paddle
board; a spicy cloud
of hashish wafts around

Mr. Ripley; he lies
there, defiant; on other
shores, people are barbequing,
drinking, smoking Turkish hookahs,

or partying; young rascals
climb into a tree
overhanging the water and
jump in from atop

the canopy shimmying along
a rope, roaring, snorting,
intoxicating themselves on their
vitality; others reading or

writing in hammocks stretched
between the trees; on
the seemingly endless shore
I hear so many

languages, see so many
skin colors, from the
garden gate of a
villa-like property comes an

elderly lady in a
bathrobe, hangs it in
a tree, and sinks
into the lake, at

her usual entry spot,
as she smilingly explains
to me, and glides
away; three Italian women

are having trouble navigating
their rowboat; the manager
of the boat rental
company eventually pulls them

back resolutely with a
long hook, into one
of the bays; the
whole thing accompanied

by a lot of
laughter, lightness of being,
as if it were
the *Gulf of Naples*.

Grasping Complex Urban Spaces

Growing up in Paris,
as the son of
a French mother and
a German father, or

perhaps the other way
around; he sits in
Reichenberger Street, not far
from *Kottbusser Tor*, and

smokes; Berlin, its wide-branching
urban spaces, inspire him,
the two-room apartment is
simple, he still has

a studio, where he
works as a freelancer;
design, graphics, film, media,
and he smokes, and

takes breaks; practical things
to do with my
stay here, are for
him only briefly, marginally,

of importance; he looks
at the urban whole;
in the hall hangs
a reproduction of Picasso,

a man and a
woman, drawn by the
artist, making love, reclining,
rapt; my host seems

at one with space
and time; everyday worries
do not penetrate his
thoughts; *many are overwhelmed*

by Berlin's size, he
believes, *and after an
initial euphoria they eventually
move away again*, he

says, *they can't grasp
such complex urban spaces.*

To Be a *Flâneur* in Berlin, Inspired by Benjamin

To fathom a metropolis
like Berlin is to
be a *flâneur*, like
Walter Benjamin was, decades

ago in Paris; in
a very suggestive way
he brought strolling, as
a form of existence

and cognition, to its
full glory for the
first time, a suggestive
narrative, which to this

day still arouses deep
longings in us and
impels us on; *The
Arcades Project*, born from

this, remained unfinished and
only through happy circumstance
was the collection of
German and French notes

preserved; in 1933, as
a Jewish intellectual, Benjamin
went from Berlin to
Paris, and in 1940,

while fleeing from the
advancing German troops in
the French-Spanish border
town of *Port Bou,*

took his own life;
in *The Arcades Project*
there is a chapter
about the *flâneur* and

strolling; the text remains
fragmentary, a mix of
quotations and his own
thoughts; the themes are

the laissez-faire of
the flâneur, his idleness,
his slow meandering through
the streets, his hesitation

and waiting, the indecisiveness
and indeterminacy of the
flâneur, his observations of
the people, of the

market, of the whole
urban hustle and bustle
of the flâneur of
the night, of course

also his loneliness; the
principle of being a
flâneur; for Proust and
Baudelaire, strolling as an

art of philosophical walk,
soaking up the present
of the metropolis, and
guiding the flâneur into

a vanished time; Benjamin
says that *Paris first*
conceived the flâneur and
that strolling is based

on the notion that
the reward for idleness,
is more valuable than
that of work, because

the flâneur studies life.[12]

---

[12] Benjamin, 1999; pp. 416-455

References

Benjamin, W. (1999). *The Arcades Project*. Cambridge, MA; London: The Belknap Press of Harvard University Press.

Beachy, R. (2015). *Gay Berlin. Birthplace of modern identity*. New York: Vintage Books.

Broecher, J. (2000). A didactic approach emphasising the social habitat as an attempt to meet growing social disintegration: Teaching in classes with youth of conspicuous behaviour using aesthetic and cultural means of communication. *Disability & Society, 15*(3), 489-506, https://doi.org/10.1080/713661965, Link.

Broecher, J. (2015a). Inspirational moments in an educator's life: It is all about responsible relationships, important learning, philosophic imagination and the will to move ahead. *Studies in Social, Emotional, and Behavioral Education, Vol. 6*. Norderstedt, Germany: Books on Demand, Link.

Broecher, J. (2015b). How David P. Weikart's HighScope Summer Camp for (Gifted) Teenagers became a sustainable model for my later work in special education and inclusive education. *Gifted Education International, 31*(3), 244-256, https://doi.org/10.1177/0261429414526655, Link.

Broecher, J. (2015c). Implementing School-Wide Positive Behavioral Interventions and Supports (PBIS) in German schools: The challenge of knowledge politics, education cultures and teacher perspectives. In B.

Higgins (Ed.), *Goal setting and personal development: Teachers' perspectives, behavioral strategies and impact on performance* (pp. 101-151). New York: Nova Science Publishers, <u>Link</u>.

Broecher, J. (2016). The long struggle to turn around an inhumane, corrupt, paramilitary school specialized for students with emotional and behavioral difficulties. In R. Nata (Ed.), *Progress in Education, Vol. 38* (pp. 39-72). New York: Nova Science Publishers, <u>Link</u>.

Broecher, J. (2019a). Teaching on the frontline. In J. Broecher, *Creating learning spaces: Experiences from educational fields* (pp. 11-40). Bielefeld: Transcript, https://doi.org/10.14361/9783839448878, <u>Link</u> (the book has been selected for *Knowledge Unlatched*, <u>Link</u>).

Broecher, J. (2019b). Maladjusted youth as sand in the gears? In J. Broecher, *Creating learning spaces: Experiences from educational fields* (pp. 41-54). Bielefeld: Transcript, https://doi.org/10.14361/9783839448878, <u>Link</u> (the book has been selected for *Knowledge Unlatched*, <u>Link</u>).

Broecher, J. (2019c). When children plan a trip on their own. In J. Broecher, *Creating learning spaces: Experiences from educational fields* (pp. 91-114). Bielefeld: Transcript, https://doi.org/10.14361/9783839448878, <u>Link</u> (the book has been selected for *Knowledge Unlatched*, <u>Link</u>).

Broecher, J. (2019d). Experiential learning across the fields. In J. Broecher, *Creating learning spaces: Experiences from educational fields* (pp. 115-150). Bielefeld: Transcript, https://doi.org/10.14361/9783839448878, <u>Link</u> (the book has been selected for *Knowledge Unlatched*, <u>Link</u>).

Bröcher, J. (2021a). Transformation von Pädagogik und Gesellschaft. In J. Bröcher, *Anders lernen, arbeiten und leben. Für eine Transformation von Pädagogik und Gesellschaft* (pp. 7-31). Bielefeld: transcript, https://doi.org/10.14361/9783839456514, <u>Link</u>.

Bröcher, J. (2021b). Das Wissen, seine Strukturen und seine Produktion. In J. Bröcher, *Anders lernen, arbeiten und leben. Für eine Transformation von Pädagogik und Gesellschaft* (pp. 33-102). Bielefeld: transcript, https://doi.org/10.14361/9783839456514, <u>Link</u>.

Bröcher, J. (2021c). Lern- und Bildungsprozesse anders entwerfen. In J. Bröcher, *Anders lernen, arbeiten und leben. Für eine Transformation von Pädagogik und Gesellschaft* (pp. 103-121). Bielefeld: transcript, https://doi.org/10.14361/9783839456514, Link.

Bröcher, J. (2021d). Transdisziplinäre Studien in der Metropole Berlin: Visuelle Spiegelungen. In J. Bröcher, *Anders lernen, arbeiten und leben. Für eine Transformation von Pädagogik und Gesellschaft* (pp. 123-151). Bielefeld: transcript, https://doi.org/10.14361/9783839456514, Link.

Bröcher, J. (2021e). Filmanalyse als Kultur- und Gesellschaftsanalyse. In J. Bröcher, *Anders lernen, arbeiten und leben. Für eine Transformation von Pädagogik und Gesellschaft* (pp. 153-182). Bielefeld: transcript, https://doi.org/10.14361/9783839456514, Link.

Bröcher, J. (2021f). Das ländliche Westdeutschland zur ersten Hälfte des 20. Jahrhunderts: Soziokulturelle Rekonstruktionen. In J. Bröcher, *Anders lernen, arbeiten und leben. Für eine Transformation von Pädagogik und Gesellschaft* (pp. 183-208). Bielefeld: transcript, https://doi.org/10.14361/9783839456514, Link.

Bröcher, J. (2021g). „Bodies under Glass": Erkundungen in virtuellen Räumen. In J. Bröcher, *Anders lernen, arbeiten und leben. Für eine Transformation von Pädagogik und Gesellschaft* (pp. 209-222). Bielefeld: transcript, https://doi.org/10.14361/9783839456514, Link.

Bröcher, J. (2022a). *Berlin-Passagen, Cultural Mapping und transdisziplinäre Erkundungen im urbanen Raum. Notizen, zwischen Feldtagebuch und Lyrik.* Norderstedt: Books on Demand, Link.

Bröcher, J. (2022b). *Lebenswelt und Didaktik. Unterricht mit sogenannten „verhaltensauffälligen" Jugendlichen auf der Basis ihrer (alltags-)ästhetischen Produktionen* (2nd rev. ed.). Heidelberg: Universitätsverlag Winter, https://doi.org/10.33675/2022-82538577, Link.

Broecher, J. (2023a). *Tomasz: Notes on future ways of learning, working, and living. Educational projects and experiences on a farmstead in Anhalt, Eastern Germany.* Norderstedt, Germany: Books on Demand, Link.

Broecher, J. (2023b). *Ludwik: Notes on future ways of learning, working, and living. Educational projects and experiences on a farmstead in Anhalt, Eastern Germany, part II*. Norderstedt, Germany: Books on Demand.

Broecher, J., Davis, J. H., Matthews, K., Painter, J. F., and Pasour, K. (2014). How transatlantic workshops and field trips can make German-American university-partnerships an active learning space. *Internationalisation of Higher Education, Vol. 2*, 18-42, https://doi.org/10.1177/02614 29414526655, Link.

Broecher, J., Davis, J. H., and Painter, J. F. (2017). Rediscovering the political dimension of the personal life story: Results from an intergenerational narrative learning project with older adults in South Westphalia. *International Journal of Lifelong Education, 36*(4), 471-485, https://doi.org/10.1080/02601370.2017.1285361, Link.

Broecher, J. and Painter, J. F. (2019). Spaces of commoning, in Berlin and other cities, and their potential for the building of sustainable social communities and educational cultures. 49th annual conference of the Urban Affairs Association (UAA): *Claiming Rights to the City: Community, Capital, and the State,* April 24–27, 2019, Los Angeles, California, Luskin Conference Center (poster presentation); ResearchGate, May 2, 2019, https://doi.org/10.13140/RG.2.2.31459.20002/1, Link.

Broecher, J. and Painter, J. F. (2021). Throwing out a net over Berlin via Airbnb bookings: Educators in search of the metropole's creative potential. In R. Nata (Ed.), *Progress in Education, Vol. 66* (pp. 99-123). New York: Nova Science Publishers, Link.

Broecher, J. and Painter, J. F. (2023). Transformative community projects in East Germany's rural spaces: Exploring more sustainable forms of learning, working, and living. *Frontiers in Sociology, Vol. 8,* 1164293, https://doi.org/10.3389/fsoc.2023.1164293, Link.

Broecher, J., Painter, J. F., Davis, J. H., and Williams, A. (2017). Professional growth through guided autobiographical reflection: A case study from pre-service teacher education. In R. Nata (Ed.), *Progress in Education, Vol. 43* (pp. 153-196). New York: Nova Science Publishers, Link.

Burgess, R. C. (1991). *In the field: An introduction to field research*. London, New York: Routledge.

Davidson, J., Bondi, L., and Smith, M. (2017). *Emotional geographies* (first published by Ashgate Publ., 2005). London, New York: Routledge.

Denzin, N. K. and Lincoln, Y. S. (2011). *The SAGE handbook of qualitative research* (4th ed.). Los Angeles, London: Sage.

Duxbury, N., Garrett-Petts, W. F., and MacLennon, D. (Eds.) (2015). *Cultural mapping as cultural inquiry*. New York, London: Routledge.

Feyerabend, P. (2010). *Against method: Outline of an anarchistic theory of knowledge* (4th ed., first release 1975). London, New York: Verso.

Florida, R. (2002). *The rise of the creative class: ...and how it's transforming work, leisure, community, & everyday life*. New York: Basic Books.

Florida, R. (2005). *Cities and the creative class*. New York, London: Routledge.

Gay, P. (2002). *Weimar culture: The outsider as insider*. New York, London: W. W. Norton & Co.

Kerr, A. (1997). *Wo liegt Berlin? Briefe aus der Reichshauptstadt* (3rd ed.). Berlin: Aufbau-Verlag.

Roberts, L. (Ed.). (2012). *Mapping cultures. Place, practice and performance*. New York: Palgrave Macmillan.

Sendra, P. and Sennett, R. (2020). *Designing disorder. Experiments and disruptions in the city.* London, New York: Verso.

Sennett, R. (1992). *The uses of disorder. Personal identity and city life* (reprint of the 1970 ed.). New York, London: W. W. Norton.

Sloterdijk, P. (2011). *Spheres I: Bubbles*. South Pasadena, CA: Semiotext(e)

Sloterdijk, P. (2014). *Spheres II: Globes*. South Pasadena, CA: Semio-text(e)

Sloterdijk, P. (2016). *Spheres III: Foams*. South Pasadena, CA: Semio-text(e)

Toczyski, P., Broecher, J., and Painter, J. F. (2022). Pioneers of German-Polish inclusive exchange: Jaczewski's and Kluge's Europeanization in education despite the Iron Curtain. *Prospects: Comparative Journal of Curriculum, Learning, and Assessment, 52*(3-4), 567-583, https://doi.org/10.1007/s11125-021-09545-x, Link.

Broecher, J. and Painter, J. F. (2021)

Throwing out a Net over Berlin via Airbnb Bookings: Educators in Search of the Metropole's Creative Potential

In R. Nata (Ed.), *Progress in Education, Vol. 66* (pp. 99-123)
New York: Nova Science Publishers, Open Access, Link

The paper's first section presents the goal of the documented research: to connect the creative cities discourse with the development of innovative educational cultures, with a spotlight on the city of Berlin. One particular element of this research was to examine the social and cultural worlds which have been accessed through the booking platform Airbnb over a two-year time frame. The paper's second section indicates which methodology was used and how the data were collected: 27 city-wide randomly booked places were investigated, using cultural mapping, case study, participant observation, unstructured interviewing, and listening. The results are reviewed in the third section in the form of short case descriptions. Section four discusses the findings: While a majority of hosts demonstrated diverse lifestyles and practiced openly communicative and productive economic patterns (which are connected in the literature with the creative class), a particular group also demonstrated limited financial resources and precariousness. In the paper's final section, the conclusion that the role of Airbnb in the context of urban change is more than ambivalent is discussed. This conclusion is provided despite the fact that Airbnb allows new communicative and economic forms. The Airbnb booking platform implies problematic effects on the social fabric of a city like Berlin. The paper concludes that schools should not only empower the younger generation with regard to their creative potential but that schools should also involve students in a critical analysis of urban change and challenge them to think about really sustainable forms of urban sharing.

Joachim Broecher explores Berlin's urban spaces as well as progress in building a transformative community project in Eastern Germany's Anhalt region, going on from there to discuss emotional and social geographies in Polish literature. For more about his prolific teaching and consulting in schools, universities and international venues, see https://broecher-re-search.de/